Wells of Night

by Gabriel Blanchard

Clickworks Press • Baltimore, Maryland

Copyright © 2017 Gabriel Blanchard.
Cover design © 2017 Clickworks Press.

All rights reserved.

First publication: Clickworks Press, 2017
Release: CP-WN-INT-P.IS-1.0

ISBN-10: 1-943383-29-4
ISBN-13: 978-1-943383-29-0

For exclusive updates, deals, and sneak peeks sign up at clickworkspress.com/join.

Divide and eat the lingering hours,
Consume that nourishment of light:
Drink the nectar of evening flowers,
And water from the wells of night.

*to Zion
from Penance*

with some regret and much love

Contents

Foreword .... *ix*
Sonnets 1
    I. Bonfires in autumn sunlight on cool eves
    II. Candles afloat in aisles filled with flowers
    III. To search for God, pow'r failed high fantasy
    IV. Abraham climbed the mountain with his son
    V. On the pectoral muscle and the waist
    VI. Broken with beauty in a lover's arms
Elegies 5
    The Poisonweed Man
    The Foundling
    Supernova
    The Infirmament
    Antithalamion
Lyrics 17
    The Adoration of the Image of God
    Crown Celestial
    Hymn to Insomnia
    Midnight Ballad
Færie Ball 25
Notes 37

Foreword

These poems were mostly written at different times. Although they share a good deal in terms of themes and imagery, they are about a variety of subjects, and I have made no attempt to keep my style woodenly consistent, trying rather to suit it to the subject matter and feel of the individual poem. Many deal with my experiences as a gay Catholic, striving with mixed success to live according to the Church's teaching; but those that do not obviously deal with that subject are not, as a rule, intended to—excessive 'decoding' should not be necessary.

That said, one merit of poetry is that it can be highly allusive in a compact way, and I have taken full advantage of the fact. The notes at the end are intended to disentangle some of the images. If you wish to have recourse to the notes in the course of a poem, I suggest finishing the poem first, reading the notes about it, and then rereading the poem; interrupting the flow of reading, though natural in a textbook and supportable in prose fiction, can be disastrous in verse.

These notes should not be supposed to be exhaustive, either of the poems they explore or of the sources they cite. A number of symbols I employ have other, additional meanings that I have ignored—symbolism is like that. And my debts to other poets have gone largely unsaid, though the canny reader can probably find influences from and parallels to John Donne, Christina Rossetti, Algernon Swinburne, T. S. Eliot, Kahlil Gibran, and others.

My sincere thanks go out to those who have encouraged and helped me in assembling this volume, particularly Ben Y. Faroe, Bill Hoard, Annette Goeres, Fr. Stephen Holt, Joseph Cardamone, and Aaron Brooks.

Sonnets

I

Bonfires in autumn sunlight on cool eves,
   Taking gold tea beneath a lonely oak:
   Lighthearted songs reverberate through smoke
As huddled flames whisper beneath the leaves;
A grey lake's glisten in the rising moon,
   Where the stag raises his proud crown aloft,
   A silhouette erect upon the soft
Coverlet of small flowers in the gloom;
These things and so much more slip from our hands:
   A daisy chain, the cakes we ate at tea-time,
      Almond-dark eyes and hands on bright cufflinks,
And crinolines and gloves and hats with bands—
   Thrown back as flotsam on sea waves at nighttime;
      The gulls keen to its foaming as it sinks.

II

Candles afloat in aisles massed with flowers
   Bound up with damask ribbons; the pure choir
   Chanting, engloried by the loft and spire,
Th' epithalamion to grace the bower.
The silk-gowned lady, the snow-vested priest,
   Familial faces gladly haloed there,
   The twyform sacrament, the lilied hair,
All gilt by fire from the rose-windowed east—
Not for thee, not for thee. The dream dissolves;
   The stuff of wraiths, and lost to such as thee,
      Men with inverted hearts and strange-lensed eyes.
The priest alone remains. He prays, absolves,
   And mutters, 'Everlasting chastity.'
      I bow my head and sign my breast crosswise.

III

To search for God, pow'r failed high fantasy:
    To man the will's ramparts, illuminate
    The mind, belt up the passions, cultivate
The saintly rose of male virginity—
My soul's earth was too bitter with resent
    To nourish leaf or bud save for the tare.
    Sow flesh, and it will ivy here or there,
Twist, flower, fruit, and die, its effort spent.
The war of sense with soul is child's play;
    The war of soul with soul, a fearful thing:
        Join battle evening, morning, noon, and night,
No respite here from the relentless fray.
    I flinch (desire itself a nettle's sting),
        And cry, 'Would I were guiltless for scant light!'

IV

Abraham climbed the mountain with his son,
    Hand in forsaken hand, his heart aflame
    With knightly faith in the all-holy Name
Unspeakable, Its strange will to atone.
My heart, my love, I had vowed me to slay,
    Amid psalms sung with censed and ardent weight,
    Deep gleams of gold—pomps of the virgin state
Oblate to God, His command to repay.
My faith was shattered with a filthy kiss.
    With passionate swell, the gleaming heat flowed out
        Of my fierce heathen heart: ah, I could not
Take up the knife to plunge it in my bliss.
    So down the mountain to perpetual drought
        I wandered, tied by that bitter love knot.

V

On the pectoral muscle and the waist
   Slide fiery fingers; to the dark, sweet stars
   Bare their beauty, and twine my lips with yours,
Arms and strong shoulders, touch and sound and taste.
Look down from holy Mary's statued pose
   And from the pierced and flaming Sacred Heart;
   Hymnodic voice, skin silk or sculptor's art,
Breath incense on my throat like damask rose—
I seem to swoon, as I were drugged or dreaming,
   And rest then in the sabbath of our glow.
     Do I now sell the feathers of the Dove
Only to scent and touch such transient seeming?
   It is appointed we be judged, I know,
     Yet cannot bear to lose love e'en for Love.

VI

Broken with beauty in a lover's arms,
   Sweetly distressed and stricken down by pleasure,
   Exalted by pains splendorous past measure—
And then collapsing in his salt night-charms.
Sleep comes and goes; the moon looks through the veil
   Drawn round incensate touches in the dark.
   Fingers on drowsing skin can feel his spark
Of icon-deity, with sweat grown stale.
Is this my heart's desire, this my delight?
   I turn to face my own edge of the bed
     And bitterly think how the god has flown,
While he, Thy substitute this single night,
   Sleeps on. My prayers are rich with things unsaid.
     With Thee, without Thee, I am yet alone.

Elegies

The Poisonweed Man

I met a man with night-lit eyes,
Rough fingertips, tight-lipped and wise.
He tore the clasps clean off his shirt,
Displayed a ribcage full of dirt,
   And said to me, *5*
     'This is of thee
     A portrait true.'
I did not heed.
I flung him upward, through the voidy blue,
And went about my each affair *10*
With burnished teeth and burnished hair.

The man returned. He floated down,
He came to me through twilight brown,
Hung by my window heavily;
Nightly he eyed me steadily. *15*
   He whispered, 'There,
     The roots lay bare,'
     And pointed in.
I cursed and sware.
I broke the glass, I cried, 'I have no sin,' *20*
And went about my daily work.
Felt nothing in my ribcage lurk.

In my bedroom the rough man stopped,
When desperate cloudbursts dripped and dropped,
To find me; said, 'I warn you, friend, *25*
Consider.' Brandished forth the ends
   Of leaves black-red
   Like bloodied lead
   Burgeoning out
(I tossed in bed), *30*
From that heart's rotten soil to fume and sprout.
With fear I writhed, with horror wept—
Then chose to mock, and turned, and slept.

The sunlight broke into my room.
I rose and mocked again, said, 'Doom?' *35*
A voice spoke close beside my ear:
'Thy fate has come on thee,' he sneered.
   Looked at my hands:
   With vine-leaf bands
   Torn, raw, and red— *40*
Such dirty hands.
I screamed, I sought the mirror by my bed
And saw a face tight-lipped and wise
With earth-stained chest and night-lit eyes.

The Foundling

Black sky above, black snow below:
Unsoiled, untouched, unlit this moonless night.
Dry wind sweeps wide, gasps cold against
My eyes and stings like fire, my hands and stings like fire.

What universe, blasphemous with vacated space,   *5*
Could issue in such diabolic night?
Ruthless, sleepless, lifeless,
Lacking all shelter, as bereft of heat
As though it were the veiled face of some netherworld planet
Expelled from the golden circles of our home's heart?   *10*

A thin cry tears the wind, keening, tearing,
So weakly sent from the horizon.
My frostbitten feet pound the snow; frozen fingers
Clench themselves in effortly fists.

Nestled in a hollow of the snow   *15*
Lies a raw red mark in the deep frost:
A boy, a child, naked as birth,
Skin sliced like a lamb for slaughter, scarlet all over
Like the margin of an illuminated missal,
Lying beneath these sacrilegious heavens.   *20*

I stoop to touch, weeping, stooping,
Reaching to the raw innocent weakly.
He whispers to me, wits drugged with chill, flesh charred
With unabsolving cold. I stoop in close to hear.

'And now you take an interest?   *25*
Page upon page of ink, shade, shape, and color,
Thrown back like flotsam on the moaning surf—
I myself have forgotten half of them—
And now you take an interest, now,
You *hypocrite lecteur*, you, you …'   *30*

I took him in my arms; the lament continued,
Too weak to hear beneath the gasping wind.
His flesh was cold on mine, worn red and thin,
But the alarm lay in the ice-blue face.

No boyish face upon that little body. *35*
Too worn with care, too shorn of ignorance,
It was as worn and weathered as my own; it was like my own.
I looked about. No house, no road, no light,
No sign of safety and no source of help.
I pressed him close and wept frustrated grief. *40*

Then a bronze bell tolled, far off in the night:
Summoning the living, mourning the dead, proclaiming that the hour is late.
I rose, and shapes rose in the darkness with me
And stalked me as I made our way toward it.

Supernova

> *Then the devil taketh him up into the holy city, and setteth him on a pinnacle of the temple, and saith unto him, If thou be the Son of God, cast thyself down: for it is written, He shall give his angels charge concerning thee: and in their hands they shall bear thee up.*
> —The Gospel According to Saint Matthew, 4.v-vi

Hey there, kid,
Congratulations:
You're gonna be a star.

You have no idea the glory you set yourself up for
When you took your leave of the angels given charge over you 5
To stride out into the wide open heavens
From the high bell-tower, the pinnacle of Saint Sebastian's;
No idea the fabulous colors that would spread like water
Beneath the stained glass, shining scarlet.

The reverend ministers of the Absolute will be there, 10
With their brimstone Bibles and their focused families,
To pity your star-crossed life, and pity more
That world that sent you down there:
The great Gomorrah, licensing your lifestyle;
And they will shake their grave, sagacious heads 15
Over the depravity, the perversion, the corruption
That possessed you to take your final flight from darkness into darkness.
And your lukewarm, scarlet flesh will be a sermon,
An advertisement for virtue, a commercial for purity
(Didn't I tell you that you'd be a star?); 20
And they will raise a monument over your hideous heart,
Bearing the cruciform inscription:
Another victim of a night in Sodom.

Congratulations, boy:

You've hit it big time, 25
You've hit primetime pavement hard; you're a star.

And the rainbow angels will act up there,
Bearing glad banners and shouting *Stones for bread* through megaphones,
To pity your star-crossed life, and pity more
That world that sent you down there: 30
The bully pulpit, repressing your truth;
And they will wag their jeweled and painted faces
Over the silence, the subjugation, the judgment
That seduced you to take your final flight from darkness into darkness.
And your hot, scarlet body will be an editorial, 35
An advertisement for openness, a commercial for tolerance
(I told you, right, that you'd be a star?);
And they will erect a monument over your horrified heart,
Bearing the triangular inscription:
Another victim of the might of Rome. 40

You have no idea the glory you set yourself up for—
All the networks of the world, and the glory of them;
The teleprompted tug-of-war (fear not, the very sinews of your corpse are numbered);
The righteous waging holy war against the righteous
Upon your battlefield body 45
Below the stained glass, shimmering scarlet.

Hello there, son:
What a thrill, for your last few seconds, to know
You're gonna be a sta

The Infirmament

Boy lost and lonely,
I fell for him like a sparrow plummeting from the heavenly air,
And ran my fingers through his heavenly hair,
Counting each strand.
I played the hymn of my joy upon the harp-strings of his
    veins;   *5*
I kissed the scars that lay on his flesh like flowers
Because, to me, they were beautiful.
Hand in hand, everything was beautiful.
He was the night wrapped round me like a cloak,
He was the murmur of music, the smell of the sea,   *10*
He was my chapel to the blissful Trinity.

When the angels bore him on their weeping wings away from
    me,
That early day of the raw, newborn year, the nightmare year,
Then was I devout—loving—holy.
I took up my cross and bravely bore it,   *15*
Despising the shame.
Even when I stumbled under its weight,
Never did I cease to pour my perfume on Thy feet.

But the lonely hours rattled in the skull,
Like trash whispering on the pavement of rain-dampened alleys
    where the wind breathes   *20*
Below a numb sky punctured by apartment towers,
    steeples, and skyscrapers.
Insomnia dripped against the doors and windows.

Lord, I am not worthy that Thou shouldest come under my roof,
So I have barred the door;
I hear Thee knock, and do my daily work,   *25*
Choking back tears for me, Thee, him.
My tapers smoulder and are not quenched.
I am emptied, overshadowed, noughted;

A bitter-lovely peace lies over me.

I beat the sunlight with one fractured wing, *30*
Spinning, spiraling, plummeting,
Feathers aflame with loves, wax dripping into the sea
So many miles beneath.
Baptize me into death
And not resurrection, I beg of Thee; *35*
Thou art no necromancer: let the dead bury their dead.

Callest me to some strange, angelic state?
I tried to be his seraph,
Twin to his loveliness, the shade beneath his tree,
The star of his night and the salt of his sea. *40*
But he has been concealed from me
By the wings of One and another—
Thou killest every thing I love from me.
I have wandered on corrupt wings through the night,
Playing the husband; playing the whore; *45*
Never more lonely and lost than when I touch strange lovelinesses.
He is as invisible to me as Thee.
Let me fall, let me drown,
Please.

And in my locked and vacant heart *50*
I yet adore Thee;
With tears and rages, I blaspheme the call,
And when I fall,
I fall before Thee.

Antithalamion

Study me then, you who shall lovers bee
At the next world, that is, at the next Spring,
  For I am every dead thing
  In whom love wrought new Alchimie.
—John Donne

Love is the most terrible of the gods.
Those deities whose demesne is among passions or pleasures
Are scarcely more than sprites or river-gods
When shaken by the crashing of the ambrosial curls of Love.
Beauty has mastering force in its subtle hands; *5*
Truth seems almighty when at first you meet it,
Prostrate before dispassioned clarity,
Unmoved and moving; nonetheless,
Love is the older and the stronger power.
Love twines through every other thing: *10*
Through breath and warmth and light, secretly
He insinuates himself through every vein, nerve, and sinew,
Releasing nothing, no one from his grasp.
The murmur that enchants the drowsing lover
In the drugged, dreaming hours perfumed with heat; *15*
The Orphic voice, ringing jewel-clear among the entangling
    flowers;
The divine thundering, above dread Ocean's face, below the
    hieratic stars:
None is afore, or after other,
None is greater, or less than another.
Love's single voice rings through, *20*
Breaking the cedars.

Yes, God is Love, though the word sticks in the throat.
I have known Love
As the honeyed scroll embittering the entrails,
As the devouring fire that terrified the sons of Israel *25*
And was silent to the mantled gaze of Elijah.

I have drunk deep, deep of the fountain of the Spirit
And been cast out by the Spirit into the wilderness,
Its nights without fire,
Its days empty and alien. *30*
I have wandered the dunes and wadis of the pathless waste and eaten of the stones;
I have fallen, fallen from the uttermost pinnacle of the Temple;
I have beheld all the kingdoms of the world, and the glory of them,
And behind them, as in a glass darkly, a strange pair of horns.
I too have sat outside the great city, *35*
Unable to discern between my right hand and my left
While the gourd curled up about my head,
Only to wither in a blast of pentecostal wind.
I too have mourned the pillar of salt, blasphemed among the potsherds and the ashes,
Seen the ram tangled in the thicket only when my hands were already drenched in scarlet. *40*

I laid myself on the floor of Ocean,
Arms crossed for blessing over my breast,
And listened to the cold drums of the saltwater
Beat sadly against the torn rocks, seven miles overhead.
I chanted my hymn to Love *45*
As I breathed deeply of the seaweed and feasted upon the old, black earth;
And I was no one to the whale and Leviathan took no heed,
So that I myself was drawn out with a hook—assumed
From the shelter where I had fallen, from the bowels of the brine.
Risen into open air, I stared at the stars, *50*
Shaking before the dread eyes of the heavens which were given charge over me.
And there I heard an Orphic voice, crying,
'Come up here, and I shall show thee what is to take place after this,
Not by conversion of the Godhead into flesh,
But by taking of that Manhood into God.' *55*

The pentecostal blast returned, and clave the sea in two;
The fundament of Ocean was laid bare,
Dry as bones in the wilderness.
The earth shook. The heavens were parted
And rolled up, like a scroll that snaps back to its accustomed
    spiral   *60*
After the fracture of its final seal.
Suspended between earth and sea and sky, in the midst of the
    Throne
I saw the seven holy Eyes, and knew
That like the ancient prophetess, my sister,
I would never be believed when I preached to the bones
    and the breath,   *65*
Because I had spurned the divine Bridegroom
To whom I promised my naked soul and body.
Bowing, I pulled my mantle over my head,
And murmured, 'Blessed be the name of the Lord.'

All this, all this is written in the terrible book of Love.   *70*
Had Cassandra or the Sibyl or Elijah forewarned me,
I might have refused to sell my soul to God,
Forborne to write my name in Blood
Most Precious, forsworn the incanted vows and cursings—
Might, might; too late.   *75*
The Book of Life lies open, its pages red and wet
(The wounded Hands bleed everlastingly);
The whispered vows are broken, yet persist,
Renewing themselves, flowering from every vein, nerve, and
    sinew;
Already I know the savor of heaven.   *80*
If I could want what I would want,
I should be holy even now.

'Sovegna vos a temps de ma dolor,'
Poi s'ascose nel foco che gl'affina.

This is the faith, which,   *85*
Except a man keep, whole and entire,
He cannot be saved.

LYRICS

The Adoration of the Image of God

Words fail me.
Hair like brown twisted wild reeds
That grow in pure wide lonely places
To shimmer in the sun, in the heart's heat.
Your bones, your skin are white rock—
Marble, alabaster, pearl, such small names
For an archetype incarnate.
Teach sculptors, painters, doctors, architects
To know proportion, balance, and perfection.
I can feel, I would feel
The warmth of your chin on the back of my hand,
The faintest abrasion against your skin on the tips of my fingers
As I brush by your lip, lingering;
I can smell your scent, your salt, the heat of your hair,
I taste your eyelids (*turn away thine eyes from me, for they
    have overcome me*);
Words fail me.

Grey sapphires look back at me, and I am a brown twisted wild
    reed.

The shape of your shoulder, the pulse of your chest,
Ideal and actual, beauty (*these signs are what they signify*).
The gentle skin where the lips shut sucking
At an image of life, twining sighs of life that moves with the
    passion of dying,
Bronze belly, lips and hands traverse muscle, muscle, muscle
Obediently; rejoice (*again I say, rejoice*);
Hips sliding on their stone unbreakable frame, words fail me,
Smooth hairs and sinews, strong, beautiful;
Your strength is here,
Your strength that is weakness, the strength that sums us up
In a concrete passionate act, heat to heat,
Exposing our innermost desires—the wand that lifts the veil of
    our mystery.

Your sex erect, yearning, daring,   *30*
Wishing and fearing to be known:
For to be known in nakedness is to be loved or hated,
And to be wounded in this fleshly head is to be wounded in the heart of the spirit.

Grey sapphires look back at me, and you are a brown twisted wild reed.

I would pour out my love, my adoration of the image of God, but   *35*
Words fail me;
I bury my head in you, bury your head in me,
Your strength is worthy, your beauty is holy,
I would say with every touch taste smell and look.
I receive your weakness into me because you are strong,   *40*
I receive your strength into me because you are need.

Nothing suffices. I see no other way
Worthily to worship your beauty, I cannot refrain
From wishing to possess feel sleep beside you inside you around you
Masculine maculate immaculate glory,   *45*
Incarnate archetype.

Jesus Christ.
What have we done? What have I done?
He looks just like You.

They all do.   *50*

Crown Celestial

The world was in its winter; in the lands
Burnt by sunrise, east of the inner sea,
The angel-haunted Holy City lay
Upon its starlit, olive-woven peaks.
There an unlikely forted palace housed   *5*
The heir of Solomon's regalia:
Though of uncertain birth to bear the crown,
He came in golden clouds of frankincense;
He ruled his people with an iron rod,
And crafted a new Temple to the Lord,   *10*
For which he was reviled by Israel.
Weeping for loss, he cried, 'I am your king,
I and no other'; but they did not heed,
Though many shed their blood on his account,
Purpling the streets of Zion, Bethlehem,   *15*
Yea, all Judæa and the lands about,
Massy with lilies dropping nectared tears
That coldly shone in the crescented night.
This royal shape, heir of the ancient glory,
Remembered yearly these two thousand years   *20*
By holy Church, was Herod, named the Great.

There also, in a cave beneath the earth,
Warmed by cows' breath and rested in their trough,
Straw puncturing his foster-father's hands
As his young Mother, white against the soil,   *25*
Lay back to catch her breath and loose her breast,
Lay God: the God who, by his pure command,
Brought forth those skies, burning with infant stars;
He who brought Jewry from Egyptian might
To this glade 'twixt the River and the Sea;   *30*
Yea, he who roared from his myrrhed Temple's seat.
For from this point, creation drew its breath:
He entered it, and, by his entering, made
The door-posts and the lintel, wet with blood,

The feast within, the broad desert without, *35*
The cave, the cows, the donkeys, ewes, and lambs,
The kindly earth, the wild, singing heavens,
And every rank of minds invisible
That bear them all upon their glassy wings.
Here past and future flowed, from this bright point, *40*
Being created by the birth of Meaning;
Now space threw forth fold after generous fold,
Given a center after centuries
Of aching void.

              And God opened his eyes
And murmured to his Mother as he drank *45*
Of that sweet milk. The heavens clustered close,
Transfigured into earthly charities,
And earth shone back, bright with divinity.

Hymn to Insomnia

Abroad upon a starlit summer's night,
Unshod and shirtless in the fragrant dark,
The grey wind keeps me warm: it slowly stirs
The honeysuckles' scent and roses' leaves
   Around my solitary pipe,   *5*
   Whose smoke flows over sidewalks marked
By detritus of men's more joyful evenings
Beneath revolving planetary lights.

Restless indoors and restless in the gloaming,
My brain trudges with a remorseless tread: *10*
Consider, so: this match that we have struck,
Is its bright being best illuminated
   By Thomist notions of the fact,
   Ideals of Platonic cast,
Or some modern ontology, that sold   *15*
Its birthright for a pot of gasoline?

Plato would say that fire is not fire;
An icon, in the night of earth's broad being,
Of that true flame whose being is divine—
Its very light a shade, its heat but smoke.   *20*
   (Inhale, and shake the match out, so.)
   But the Cherubic Doctor, he
Would say that fire indeed is fire, and more:
A low link in the great gold Chain of Being,

Matter suffused with God, from primal Chaos   *25*
Through element to stone, plant, beast, man, angel,
Unto that summit of created things
That wears the form of a Woman: all reveal
   Beauty by unique excellence.
   Yet centuries of nocturnal stars,   *30*
Five hundred years in their cold houses, staring
Upon half-naked forms of sleepless men,

Have driven men to madness in the dark.
The fire has left the workshops and the presses,
The forum—but that flame died long ago— *35*
And half the schools and solemn hearths and chapels
   Crouch low beneath the moon, or drowse,
   Wits bathed in wine, or huddle close
To embers in tinfoil swaddling bands.
(My pipe is out; I fetch another match.) *40*

Yet who knows but that, in these vigilant hours,
Insomnia may yet reward her cult
Of suppliants (I least of their apostles)
With some dim vision of Reality,
Through grey smoke and grey wind, shifted aside *45*
Like veils, to some brain intoxicate
With old philosophy—some wink from heaven,
    Epiphany of where that holy flame burns on,
    And how, Promethean-wise, it might be snatched again.

Midnight Ballad

In thy mad midnights, O my love,
    Beneath unhallowed stars,
Thy fingers stain thy sacred flesh,
    Painting protesting scars.

Each blade burns in my eyes and heart: *5*
    Thine unrelenting hand
No longer wounds thyself alone;
    For love drew cord and band

About us both, and tied the twain
    Into one heart, one soul.   *10*
Make me thy health, thy peace and rest,
    Ah, let me make thee whole.

For I would heal each bleeding smart
    In our soft midnight hours:
Would turn the tears to diamonds,   *15*
    And change the flames to flowers.

Færie Ball

Færie Ball

Little Lucy lay in bed
And tucked her doll close underneath her chin;
Mama and Papa kissed her golden head,
And the dark nimbus of her handsome twin.
'Sleep well, sleep tight, forget the Moon,' said Mama; *5*
'The Virgin keep your souls; no monsters bite,
Nor mischief-making færies in the room.'
Smiled at their girl and boy, linked hands with Papa,
Put out the lamp and closed them in the gloom.

Then Lucy turned, and to her brother said, *10*
'O Tommy, O Tommy,
Let's go and be jolly!
Both Mama and Papa believe us in bed;
No nodding here! we are awake.
That window is not fast to night; *15*
I have no fright; open the glass.
We two shall range out to the moor
And we shall see the færies' flight,
Drow, sylphs, and sirens silvern-white,
All dancing, dancing in the dark Moon's light.' *20*

But Tommy was agog, aghast:
'We ought not toy with Mama so;
Were our beds empty in the dawnlight,
Her heart would drown with woe;
Our Papa's grave affection, we *25*
Ought to revere more solemnly.
We have no business with Good Folk clad in poppies,
With hairy dwarves, gnomes roaming under Earth,
Or vine-drest sprites with foam along their wake,
However fair, however jolly. *30*
Mortals must 'ware a goblin's thoughts of mirth,
And were we seized by dryad, hag, or elves,
Or dragged down darkly into dwarvish delves,

How would Papa and Mama know?'

But Lucy said, 'Fie for a craven, Tommy;   *35*
You vex me so!
You are too wary;
We should make merry;
You should behold a færie.
The full-Mooned heaven bright tonight   *40*
Lights up the homeward path tonight.
There is no need for fright tonight.
Tonight, there is a færie ball,
And we twain are invited,
For I met a sprite last night   *45*
Where the green hill is mushroom-crownéd.
His fingers in the Moon were bright,
His locks dripped sap as black as night,
Elder-beard færie,
Starry-eyed and foxglove-crowned and merry.   *50*

'"Why have you left your bed?
Sure your mother worries so;
Young maidens must not tread where mushrooms grow."
I begged his pardon, made a curtsey, said,
"I only wished to see the elvish light."'   *55*

'Lucy,' broke in Tommy,
'That was foolhardy!
Don't you recall the story Papa told
Of immemorial undines, seeking brides
To grant them souls and lift them from the tides   *60*
They dwell in, watching Earth itself grow old?
You should not speak with elves, nor dark nor bright!
You should not leave the house at night!'

'Hush,' replied Lucy;
'Heed my fair story.   *65*
For, when he saw my humble politesse,
He grinned at me

And answered, with wizardly gentilesse,
'Come then and see, next elvish night,
Færies all together: *70*
Queen Mab and Vivien,
Sycorax, King Auberon,
Fifty-armed Ammon,
Miranda fair with Ariel
The undine, Puck, and Barghest fell,   *75*
I Bercilak, Morgan."
"How shall I know to come?" I said.
"Whenever Moon is full on heather,
Come to us; dance
Sweetly, in trance   *80*
Under the rich spell of sweet spirits' wines."
Look up now, Tommy, at the Moon
And such fair night weather:
Sure the undines are dancing with noblesse
To some shrill dwarf-pipe tune.'   *85*

Lucy opened up the sash,
Leapt into night
Quick as a flash.
She darted through the rose garden
With Tommy calling after,   *90*
Went past valerian and lily,
Went past the juniper with laughter,
Forgot the irises and holly;
Her feet brushed lilac, buttercup, carnation,
As Tommy breached the sill, ran through the garden,   *95*
Calling aloud the timeworn salutation
Of angels to the Queen above the stars.

Tommy was quick; Lucy was quicker:
Passed up the grey hill like a flicker
Of flame, bright white as foaming sea   *100*
When the sky frowns in the West,
Rouses the emerald ocean from its rest,
And wars with crags upon the spray-strewn shores,

Spurs wrath of Sea, thunder of Heaven blest,
Earth all-resistant to their mastery.   *105*
Up the dewed barrow, jewel-green and tall,
Came Lucy, dancing toward the mushroom wall,
Where poppies and narcissus grow.

'Come back, come back,' her brother cried with woe;
'Heather is damp with dew; I behold no færie;   *110*
Mama will scold us so; you need no wines
Brewed with gnomish sorceries from vines
Heavy with magic, phantasmal altogether.'

But then a heavy laugh chimed in the night:
'Færies be we; phantoms, no.   *115*
Sycorax, Morgan,
Queen Mab and Ammon,
Miranda, Puck, and Ariel,
Howling Barghest,
With Bercilak and High King Auberon.'   *120*
Blotting out the sweet starlight
Came the frames of ancient elves,
Rising from the deep gnomes' delves:
Sirens, hags, and weirdest sprites,
Undines with gem-studded harps,   *125*
Sylphs in apple-blossoms drest,
Tall dryads with bluebells and poppies tressed
Bearing hazel-wooden wands
And narcissus trumpets bright,
Hairy goblins raw and pale,   *130*
Redhood dwarves white-haired and hale,
Agog with drums and pipes for the færie ball.

Tommy saw Lucy dancing past the wall,
The charmed mushroom crown solemnized with light,
And darted to the barrier,   *135*
His heart crying to rescue her.
But as he set his foot within the ring,
A grim elf, clad in willow-weeds

With a carbuncle on his brow,
Drew close, and, in an accent sharp, *140*
Told Tommy, 'See now! get you gone!
The girl has entered this our how
By invitation—' with a ghastly grin
Continued—'now, my silly son,
You cannot enter in.' *145*
Then, brandishing a vervain leaf,
The færie gestured,
And Tommy was hurled backward, high
Beneath the moonlit, frosty sky,
And landed far back, weeping sore. *150*

But Lucy gazed astonisht more and more
How the færies were vestured,
In copper leaves, vermilion reeds,
And silver cobwebs glistening in the night.
Dryads, birchbark-clad, did spring *155*
After mischievous black sprites
Diamond-fingered, on the wing,
Around a fountain of pure færie water
Summoned from deep within the Earth
To serve the needs of sorcerous mirth *160*
By hags, with chanting and with laughter;
Surrounded too by tables laid with cakes
Of thyme and cloves and barley baked.
Goblins goggled in the moonlight
Under the power of Auberon's rich wines, *165*
Giggling and spinning to dwarvish chimes—
Such wines as never wet a mortal tongue,
Mulled with enchanted herbs and flowers:
Basil and parsley, poppy-seed,
Henbane and honeysuckle, spiced in hours *170*
Hid from the kindly Sun beneath the Earth,
Where wizened gnomes groaned in their inverse towers
Nine fathoms down, to satisfy their lust
For lifeless metals to adorn færie mirth,
Whose songs no mortal ear ever heard sung *175*

Beneath the starry-mansioned zodiac.

Dancing quickened, as Vivien
Thrummed a heavy mandoline.
Chalices of nectar black
Passed from the throne of Auberon *180*
Through the wroth arms of Ammon,
Rich with magic, rich with sin,
To sate the maddened thirst of Bercilak
(Ivy-skin færie,
Elf-pipe-voiced and moonlight-wreathed and hairy). *185*
He took Lucy by the hand
And led her through the crazy revelling;
The dwarves and dryads formed a ring
Around her and the undine bright,
Voluptuous and arrogant. *190*
He tossed her high, he drew her back,
Jigged rapidlier still,
He gave Lucy a witchly thrill.

As then her heart began to thrum,
Ariel sneered o'er elvish drum *195*
And tossed an ivory wand to Auberon.
'Now, my child,' the High King said,
'You have danced upon our sand,
Drunk the wine of our sacred, secret band.
You shall not pass again beyond the wall. *200*
For elvish magic has a cost:
You'll wed a spirit-man tonight,
All drest in vines and silver in the pale Moon's light.
Morgan le Fay will dress you,
Miranda tress you, *205*
Setting the starlight in your hair with hoarfrost;
Bercilak did request you.'

Then Lucy shook, and looked about the ring:
Saw sylphs gone mad with nectar, taking flights
Erratic; Ammon roaring for a fight; *210*

Saw Barghest with his jagged jaws and eyes
Aflame, now growling at his master's feet,
And old elder-beard Bercilak,
Locks all slimed with sable sap,
Goggling and grinning; and at last took fright. *215*

'High King,' she said,
'Let me go to bed;
Mama would worry so,
Were I to marry;
Papa's heart would drown with woe *220*
Amid færie flowers jolly.
True, I have drunk your sorcerous wine,
Gnomish grape from gnomish vine,
And danced with foxfire-crownéd Bercilak—
But I am only nine.' *225*

'Fie for a craven!' cried King Auberon.
'Treacherous ingrate! Turn your back
Upon an undine's gentilesse?
You, gobbler of goblin bread,
Guzzler of goblin wine? *230*
Ho! Puck and Ammon! bind her arms
Onto the scarlet bed!
Fetch yet, Morgan le Fay, the cobweb dress,
Drow-woven damask resinous with charms
Infused beneath the dark Moon's light. *235*
Lord Bercilak shall have a bride tonight,
He be ensouled and she ensorcelled, yes,
Although she show no humble politesse.
You, tell me "No"?
Vex me not so!' *240*

Tommy crept up again to where the wall
Held mortals back by witchcraft; could not hear
The Færie King's rebuke, but saw his dear,
His darling twin, begin to wail aloud
As elvish maidens dragged her to a bed *245*

All laid with silver curtains, cords of red;
She struggled to escape the wedding shroud.
Tommy wept sore to see her fright,
Wretched and writhing past the mushroom cloud,
And whispered, 'Virgin Mother, *250*
If you loved us ever,
Take pity on your helpless children now.'
No answer, save a distant tolling bell.

The King assumed his vine-drest place,
Jeweled his throne above their secret hill, *255*
Terrible his starry brow.
Bercilak was trimmed and tressed,
In scarlet hooded, clad in gnomish rings
Wrought in black dells full sick with sorcery.
Lucy soon was finely dressed, *260*
Crying gramercy; ivory-veiled and fair,
Her tears like pearls sparked in the full Moon's light.
The hag Sycorax brewed unearthly things
To mute her will and twist her human sight.
Maiden faces cruel and pale *265*
Formed a mocking line by Lucy:
Bridesmaids for the wedding night,
Star-clad witches bright with potions slimy.
Pipe, harp, and drum
Exulted in these sirens' sin *270*
With accents sharp
And savage, hideous din,
Till Auberon raised his wand for silence dread.
The music ceased, and then the High King said:

'Sycorax, raise the chalice to her lips, *275*
And pour the potion down her throat, that drips
With mandrake root and pomegranate seed,
With nettle leaf and belladonna weed,
Foxglove and lovage, juice and bloom of apple,
Thyme, sage, and parsley, nut and leaf of hazel, *280*
Hellebore, wormwood, asphodel,

Hypnotic henbane, vervain, poppy seed.'

The twisted sylph grabbed Lucy by her hair
And thrust the chalice underneath her chin—
But all at once, the ceremony stopped, *285*
The færies gasped, their instruments they dropped,
And shrank with terror from their sorcerous sin,
Their eyes all fixt in one unwavering stare.

Mama was standing at the mushroom crown
With Papa hand in hand; *290*
Neither one wore a smile;
Their eyes were flamed with fearless charity.
In her right hand she lifted high
Her fair and prayer-worn Rosary,
The cross cold iron and the beads of rowan, *295*
Worn smooth with prayers for both her children dear
(The færies trembled all with holy fear);
The mushrooms paled, their spell swiftly cast down.
The father's wisdom, mother's grace,
And brother's faith strode in toward Auberon, *300*
And aureoles sprang round them in the night:
Love's own white magic crowned them sacredly,
Garlanded them with gold light like the Sun
When he shines forth majestic at the dawn,
Dispersing villainies beneath his face *305*
That grinned and goggled in the soulless night.
Scents wafted from that holy family,
As of rosewood and frankincense and lily,
Of myrrh, of cedar smoke and rosemary,
Of Saint John's wort, valerian and holly, *310*
And drowned the hot aromas of their wines,
Withering dwarvish cakes and vines.

They drew close to the throne of ivory,
The silvered pride of all black magic's might,
And Mama told the Færie King: 'Your Grace, *315*
My husband woke me at the Angelus bell;

Our hearts presaged some woe:
We went to see our darlings, found them gone,
And we were worried so.
You ought not tamper with a mother's daughter, *320*
You ought not tempt her to your spellbound dance,
Nor let her taste your wines nor hear your laughter.
You have transgressed, High King, my magic wall
By asking her into your siren ball;
Bercilak, you outrage paternity *325*
With your lack of gentilesse
Making a fool of innocency:
This violence displays no true noblesse.
Therefore I shall speak now, nor hold my peace:
This wedding ceremony hence must cease. *330*
You, goblin, now release my daughter's hand.
Take back that chalice of your witchery,
Nor number her among your starlit band.'

Lucy ran, weeping,
Out through the night *335*
To Mama's keeping.
Fair, soft arms enfolded her;
Parents never scolded her,
Seeing her terror at such foolish sin
And her repentance from the heart within. *340*
But Papa laid his hand upon her back
And placed the other on his young son's head,
Hers with pure gold and his haloed with black,
And smiled at his offspring
And at the lullaby his wife was singing. *345*

Homeward they turned, with one contemptuous glance
Upon the færie people and their charms—
Against a mother, powerless to harm,
At a father's glance ebbing like the tide,
Or sure as shades dissolve in Daystar's light. *350*
Thus full of grace and crystal-clear of sight,
Free, they descended down the barrow deep,

Bright gold with radiance from love inside
Whose prayer dispensed the need for lamp to light,
Whose kiss breaks every spell of magic sleep. *355*

NOTES

Sonnets

II

l. 2: *damask* usually refers to a type of figured cloth (often used in religious vestments and decorations), typically made of silk or linen; it can also refer to the Damascus, or Castilian, rose, and by extension to certain shades of pink. Both the flower and the fabric take their name from the city of Damascus.

l. 4: an *epithalamion* (more commonly *epithalamium*) is a poem written in honor of a wedding, and particularly of the bride.

III

l. 1: cf. *Paradiso* XXXIII.133-145.

l. 9: cf. *Idylls of the King*, 'To the Queen,' ll. 36-38:
> ... *accept this old imperfect tale,*
> *New-old, and shadowing Sense at war with Soul,*
> *Ideal manhood closed in real man[.]*

IV

passim: cf. Genesis 22.

l. 3: cf. the 'knight of faith' described by Kierkegaard:
> *Deeper natures never forget themselves and never become something other than they were. So the knight will remember everything; but the memory is precisely the pain, and yet in his infinite resignation he is reconciled with existence. His love for the princess would take on for him the expression of an eternal love, would acquire a religious character, be transfigured into a love for the eternal being which, although it denied fulfillment, still reconciled him once more in the eternal consciousness of his love's validity in an eternal form that no reality can take from him. ... [H]e infinitely renounces the claim to the love which is the content of his life; he is reconciled in pain; but then comes the marvel, he makes one more movement, more wonderful than anything else, for he says, "I nevertheless believe that I shall get her, namely on the strength of the absurd,*

*on the strength of the fact that for God all things are possible."
... It is not the same as the improbable, the unexpected, the unforeseen. The moment the knight resigned he was convinced of the impossibility, humanly speaking; that was a conclusion of the understanding ... Faith is therefore no æsthetic emotion, but something far higher, exactly because it presupposes resignation; it is not the immediate inclination of the heart but the paradox of existence. ... So let us either forget all about Abraham or learn how to be horrified at the monstrous paradox that is the significance of his life, so that we can understand that our time like any other can be glad if it has faith.*

(From *Fear and Trembling*, 'Problemata: Preamble From the Heart.')

VI

l. 11: cf. the tale of Cupid and Psyche, related by Apuleius in *Metamorphoses, or the Golden Ass*, esp. V.20-24.

Elegies

The Poisonweed Man

l. 20: cf. I John 1.8-10.

The Foundling

l. 30: cf. Charles Baudelaire's 'To the Reader' ll. 33-40, in *Flowers of Evil*. T. S. Eliot uses the phrase at the end of the opening segment of *The Waste Land*.
ll. 41-42: cf. the epigraph at the head of Friedrich Schiller's *Song of the Bell*: *Vivos voco. Mortuos plango. Fulgura frango*. ('I call the living. I mourn the dead. I break the thunderbolts.')

Supernova

l. 7: St. Sebastian, a Christian martyr during the persecution of Diocletian (killed around 288 CE), has sometimes been half-jokingly treated as a patron of gay people. Oscar Wilde, following his release from Reading Gaol after being imprisoned for violation of sodomy laws, wandered abroad under the pseudonym *Sebastian Melmoth*.
l. 11: Focus on the Family is an evangelical Christian group that advocates for conservative public policies, especially with regard to education, marital law, and abortion. It was founded in 1977. It has been a longstanding opponent of LGBT advocacy, and supported the ex-gay movement for decades.
ll. 27-28: ACT UP (the AIDS Coalition To Unleash Power) promotes political and medical advances on behalf of those suffering from AIDS; it was founded in 1987. The group has sometimes come into conflict with the Catholic Church over its opposition to contraceptive education, notably in a 'Stop the Church' protest in 1989, in which a number of ACT UP members disrupted a Mass and one protester desecrated a Host.
GLAAD (originally the Gay and Lesbian Alliance Against Defamation, though this name is now rarely used) is a media-watchdog association that opposes negative characterizations of LGBT-identifying people.
l. 39: An equilateral pink triangle is a symbol of the LGBT movement. It originated in the Holocaust, where a pink triangle was used to mark gay

prisoners in concentration camps (of whom there were more than 50,000); LGBT activists claimed it as a symbol of pride in the 1970s.

The Infirmament

ll. 2-3: cf. Matthew 6.25-34.

l. 11: cf. John Donne's *Holy Sonnets* XIV:
> *Batter my heart three person'd God: for, you*
> *As yet but knocke, breathe, shine, and seek to mend;*
> *That I may rise, and stand, o'erthrow mee,'and bend*
> *Your force, to breake, blowe, burn and make me new.*
> *I, like an usurpt towne, to'another due,*
> *Labour to'admit you, but Oh, to no end,*
> *Reason your viceroy in mee, mee should defend,*
> *But is captiv'd, and proves weake or untrue.*
> *Yet dearely'I love you,'and would be loved faine,*
> *But am betroth'd unto your enemie:*
> *Divorce mee,'untie, or breake, that knot againe,*
> *Take mee to you, imprison mee, for I*
> *Except you'enthrall mee, never shall be free,*
> *Nor ever chast, except you ravish mee.*

l. 15: cf. Hebrews 12.1-2.

l. 17: cf. Luke 7.36-50. The unnamed woman in this passage has traditionally been identified as the Magdalene (though this interpretation has become controversial).

l. 22: quoted from the prayer *Domine Non Sum Dignus*, used immediately before the distribution of Communion, in the style of the Anglican Use: 'Lord, I am not worthy that thou shouldest come under my roof, but speak the word only, and my soul shall be healed.'

l. 24: cf. Revelation 3.20.

l. 26: cf. Matthew 12.18-21, itself quoting Isaiah 42.

l. 38: alluding to G. F. Handel's aria *Ombra Mai Fu*, which runs in part:
> *Ombra mai fu*
> *di vegetabile,*
> *cara ed amabile,*
> *soave più.*

(Never was there shade / of any plant / more dear and lovely, / nor more sweet.)

Antithalamion

Title: the reverse of an epithalamion (*vid. sup.*, note on Sonnet II.4)
Epigraph: taken from Donne's poem *A Nocturnall Upon S. Lucies Day*, written in grief for the deaths of a close friend and his daughter.
l. 4: cf. the Iliad I.679-687 (Alexander Pope's translation):
> *'Witness the sacred honors of our head,*
> *The nod that ratifies the will divine,*
> *The faithful, fix'd, irrevocable sign;*
> *This seals thy suit, and this fulfills thy vows'—*
> *He spoke, and awful bends his sable brows,*
> *Shakes his ambrosial curls and gives the nod;*
> *The stamp of Fate, and sanction of the God:*
> *High Heav'n with trembling the dread signal took,*
> *And all Olympus to the center shook.*

l. 16: Orpheus was a mythical figure whose singing was said to be so beautiful that it charmed wild beasts, and that when his wife Eurydice died of snakebite, he went down and won her back from Pluto. (The ending of this story varies; we are most familiar with the tragic version, known as early as Virgil, in which he again loses Eurydice, but other tellings had him simply victorious.) Orphism claimed to descend from Orpheus' wisdom, and offered initiation into secrets of the afterlife, including religious and magical means to be united with the gods and escape from the cycle of reincarnation in which they believed. The relationship of Orphism to Christianity was complex: on the one hand, many Orphic elements can be discerned in ancient Christian heresies, to which the orthodox were implacably hostile; on the other, Orpheus, as a figure who had gone into the underworld to rescue his beloved and returned to life, was sometimes used as a code-symbol for Christ. The emperor Severus Alexander, who was exceptionally tolerant of Christians, was reported to have statues of Abraham, Christ, and Orpheus together in his personal chapel.

ll. 18-19: cf. the *Quicunque Vult* or Athanasian Creed, which reads in part (in the translation of the Book of Common Prayer of 1662):
> *Whosoever will be saved: before all things it is necessary that he hold the Catholick Faith.*

Which faith except every one do keep whole and undefiled: without doubt he shall perish everlastingly.

And the Catholick Faith is this: That we worship one God in Trinity, and Trinity in Unity;

Neither confounding the Persons: nor dividing the Substance.

... And in this Trinity none is afore or after other: none is greater, or less than another;

But the whole three Persons are co-eternal together: and co-equal.

Once recited regularly in both Catholic and Anglican worship, the Athanasian Creed has fallen into disuse. It is still recited by some believers as a part of private prayer.

l. 21: cf. Psalm 29.

ll. 24-30: cf. Revelation 10.8-10; Exodus 19.12-18, 20.18-21; I Kings 19.9-13ff. ; Mark 1.12-13; Exodus 13.17-22.

ll. 31-34: cf. Matthew 4.1-11, Luke 4.1-13. The Gospel of Matthew (which tends to arrange material thematically rather than chronologically) reports the temptations of Christ in a different order from Luke, mounting to the climactic challenge of being offered the dominion of the whole world in exchange for worshiping the devil. When we consider Christ as the only person in the world who could have ruled the whole world with perfect justice and wisdom, the strength and significance of this temptation becomes plainer; a similar notion is presented by J. R. R. Tolkien in *The Lord of the Rings* I.ii.7, where Samwise tries to dispute Galadriel's refusal of the One Ring when Frodo offers it to her:

'But if you'll pardon my speaking out, I think my master was right. I wish you'd take his Ring. You'd put things to rights. You'd stop them digging up the gaffer and turning him adrift. You'd make some folk pay for their dirty work.'

'I would,' she said. 'That is how it would begin.'

l. 34: cf. I Corinthians 13.12.

ll. 35-38: cf. Jonah 4.

ll. 39-40: cf. Genesis 19.15-17, 23-26; Job 2.3-10; Genesis 22.1-2, 9-14, also *vid. sup.* note on Sonnet IV.3.

l. 46: cf. T. S. Eliot in *Murder in the Cathedral*, Part II, from the second choral passage:

> *I have lain on the floor of the sea and breathed with the breathing of the sea-anemone, swallowed with ingurgitation of the sponge. I have lain in the soil and criticized the worm.*

ll. 47-48: cf. Job 41.1-10.

ll. 53-55: cf. Revelation 4.1-5. Also the Athanasian Creed, in another passage:

> *For the right Faith is, that we believe and confess: that our Lord Jesus Christ, the Son of God, is God and Man:*
>
> *God, of the Substance of the Father, begotten before all worlds: and Man, of the Substance of his Mother, born in the world;*
>
> *... Who although he be God and Man: yet he is not two, but one Christ;*
>
> *One; not by conversion of the Godhead into flesh: but by taking of that Manhood into God;*
>
> *One altogether; not by confusion of Substance: but by unity of Person.*
>
> *... This is the Catholick Faith: which except a man believe faithfully, he cannot be saved.*

l. 58: cf. Ezekiel 37.1-10.

ll. 60-61: cf. Revelation 5.1-7, 8.1-5.

ll. 64-67: Cassandra, the well-known prophetess of Troy whose prophecies were always true but never believed, was said to have received her gift of foresight from Apollo. In many versions of the story, he granted her the gift in return for her promise to let him sleep with her, but after she had received it she broke her word. Enraged, but unable to withdraw a gift once given, the god added to it the curse that no one would ever believe her.

l. 71: in addition to being a prophetess in Roman culture, comparable to the Oracle of Delphi for the Greeks, the Sibyl was widely believed in Mediæval times to have foretold the coming of Christ, due to the contents of the *Sibylline Oracles*. These texts are now believed to be forgeries dating to the last centuries of the Roman Empire, and of mixed pagan, Jewish, and Christian authorship.

ll. 83-84: quoted from *Purgatorio* XXVI.147-148, and translating roughly to:

> *'Think ye betimes of how I suffer here,'*
> *Then plunged him in that fire that refines them.*

The first line is spoken to Dante by Arnaut Daniel, a fellow poet, and one of the pioneers of the troubadour movement from which Dante's own school of poetry was descended. Daniel is doing penance for his sins of lust in Purgatory; the penance of the lustful consists in running through fire, which at once purifies the souls and excites the fire of their love for God. The same lines are used in multiple poems of T. S. Eliot, notably *The Waste Land* (V.428) and *Ash Wednesday* (IV.11).

ll. 85-87: referring a third time to the Athanasian Creed, *vid. sup.*

Lyrics

The Adoration of the Image of God

l. 15: cf. Song of Solomon 6.4-10.

l. 19: cf. the Catechism of the Catholic Church, §§ 1127-1128:
> *Celebrated worthily in faith, the sacraments confer the grace that they signify. They are efficacious because in them Christ himself is at work ... The Father always hears the prayer of his Son's Church ... This is the meaning of the Church's affirmation that the sacraments act* ex opere operato *(literally: 'by the very fact of the action's being performed'), i.e., by virtue of the saving work of Christ, accomplished once for all. ... From the moment that a sacrament is celebrated in accordance with the intention of the Church, the power of Christ and his Spirit acts in and through it, independently of the personal holiness of the minister. Nevertheless, the fruits of the sacraments also depend on the disposition of the one who receives them.*

l. 20: cf. the first, second, and fourth stanzas of Algernon Charles Swinburne's poem *Laus Veneris*:

> *Asleep or waking is it? for her neck,*
> *Kissed over close, wears yet a purple speck*
>   *Wherein the pained blood falters and goes out;*
> *Soft, and stung softly—fairer for a fleck.*
> *But though my lips shut sucking on the place,*
> *There is no vein at work upon her face;*
>   *Her eyelids are so peaceable, no doubt*
> *Deep sleep has warmed her blood in all its ways.*
> *... Lo, she was thus when her clear limbs enticed*
> *All lips that now grow sad with kissing Christ,*
>   *Stained with blood fallen from the feet of God,*
> *The feet and hands whereat our souls were priced.*

l. 23: cf. Philippians 4.4.

Crown Celestial

ll.32-44: a major contrast between two schools of thought within Catholicism, Thomism (named for Thomas Aquinas) and Scotism (named for John Duns Scotus), lies in their respective approaches to the Incarnation. Thomists generally take the view that God became man to remedy sin, and that, had man not fallen, the Incarnation would not have happened. Scotists assert that the Incarnation was the plan for creation as such, without reference to the sinfulness of man—since man did in fact become corrupt, the Incarnation was also made to be the vehicle of redemption, but the Incarnation was the central act or choice of God. Some theologians work this out still further, seeing the human race as essentially the family and companions which God chose to create for himself and his Mother (e.g. Ven. Fulton Sheen's book on Mary, *The World's First Love*, and the Anglican Charles Williams' short but rich book *He Came Down From Heaven*).

Hymn to Insomnia

l. 22: although *Angelic Doctor* is a commoner epithet, St. Thomas Aquinas is sometimes called the *Cherubic Doctor*—in contrast to the *Seraphic Doctor*, St. Bonaventure. In Catholic theology, the cherubim are believed to be the second-highest order of angelic intelligences, and to know God more perfectly than any other beings, while the seraphim, the highest order, love him most perfectly (except the Blessed Virgin Mary).
l. 46: note that *intoxicate* (pronounced with the same final *a* as 'literate') is here an adjective, not a verb.

Færie Ball

ll. 18-19: *fairies* were originally so called because they were thought to be fair-skinned (in contrast to *brownies*, who were thought to be dark of skin—and universally helpful, also unlike fairies). The spelling *færie*, though not without etymological precedent, has been preferred in this poem on strictly atmospheric grounds.

Drow, now often identified with 'dark elves,' were originally a kind of water-spirit in the folklore of the Orkneys and the Shetlands.

Sylph was a term invented by the sixteenth-century alchemist Paracelsus as a word for elemental spirits of air. *Sirens* date back to classical Greece, and were believed to lure sailors to shipwreck with their incomparably beautiful singing.

l. 27: *Good Folk* was a euphemism for fairies, out of the folk belief that speaking the name of a supernatural being draws its attention (as in the proverb *Speak of the devil and he appears*). This phrase is sometimes shortened to simply 'the Folk,' and it is possible that the syllable *fox* in 'foxglove' and 'foxfire' is a corruption of *Folks'*—i.e., Folks' gloves, Folks' fire.

Poppies are the origin of opium.

ll. 28-32: *dwarves* are of course small, ugly, man-like beings associated with earth, mountains, and mines.

Gnomes are not always firmly distinguishable from dwarves, but are elementals of earth in Paracelsus' system.

Sprite is a generic term (derived through French from the Latin *spiritus*) for beings of folklore such as elves and fairies.

Goblins are first attested in the High Middle Ages, creatures similar to dwarves but more monstrous and sometimes far more minuscule.

Dryads are tree spirits (familiar to readers of the *Chronicles of Narnia* as one of that land's chief inhabitants); the English word *tree* is distantly related to the words *dryad* and *druid*.

A *hag* is an old, ugly woman, frequently a witch; whether hags are human is not always discernible. They were said to cause nightmares (hence *hagridden*) and to lurk in rivers, ponds, and marshes, waiting for children to come close so that the hags can snatch them; Jenny Greenteeth, Black Annis, and Nellie Longarms are local versions in England and Scotland.

Elves, notwithstanding the different suggestions they make to us on account of *The Lord of the Rings*, were once ambiguous and dangerous creatures, and were frequently associated with sexual threats, often connected with kidnapping. Elves played a role in culture much more like that of the modern extraterrestrial than the modern Christmas elf or the Tolkienian immortals.

The distinctions in origin and nature of the various folkloric beings mentioned in the poem are not rigorously observed.

l. 46: many species of mushroom sometimes grow in rings, occasionally many yards in diameter and often lasting years or even decades. Especially in Western Europe, these discs are called fairy rings, and are attributed in legend to the circle-patterned dancing of fairies.

l. 50: *foxgloves* are a traditional symbol of insincerity. They also contain a toxin called digitalis which, if ingested in quantity, can produce vomiting, jaundice, cardiac arrhythmia, and seizures, among other symptoms.

ll. 59-61: *undines* (an Anglicization of the Latin form *undinae*, from *unda*, 'wave') are the water elementals of Paracelsus' system, and these more or less equate to the fairies and elves of the English-speaking tradition. The idea that elves could obtain a soul by marrying a mortal is a common and variable motif in English and Celtic myth, preserved in many tales and ballads from the Mediæval period, the Renaissance, and even further on, such as *Thomas the Rymer*, the *Lai of Launfal*, and *Lady Isabel and the Elf-Knight*; in a sense, the fate of the Half-Elven in Tolkien's writings (especially of Lúthien and Arwen) could be viewed as versions of the same tradition.

ll. 71-76: *Queen Mab*, a traditional name of the queen of the fairies, appears to be an invention of Shakespeare in *Romeo and Juliet*, where she is called the midwife of dreams by Mercutio. The name is sometimes thought to derive from Medb, a legendary queen of Connacht (western Ireland).

Vivien is one of the names attributed to the Lady of the Lake in Arthurian legend (Nimue, Nyneve, and Elaine are some others).

Sycorax is another Shakespearean figure, a witch defeated by the good magician Prospero in the backstory of *The Tempest*. Any sources for her are uncertain; some scholars have connected her to Medea, though the traits they share constitute little more than both being powerfully magical feminine characters.

King Auberon as lord of the fairies (so used in *A Midsummer Night's Dream*, again by Shakespeare) may derive from Alberich, a magical character in the *Nibelungenlied* who guards the treasure of the royal house of Burgundy.

Ammon was originally the name of a nation related to the ancient Hebrews. It was used by G. K. Chesterton in his poem *Lepanto* as the name of an evil spirit; here, it is blended with the myth of the Hecatoncheires or 'hundred-handed ones,' ogreish children of Mother Earth in Greek mythology.

Miranda, another *Tempest* figure, bears a name meaning 'wondrous things' in Latin.

Ariel makes his appearance in Shakespeare after a long career as an angel (variously identified as evil or good) in Jewish and Christian folklore, poetry, and mysticism. In Milton's *Paradise Lost*, it is the name of a rebellious angel.

Puck, sometimes alternately called 'Robin Goodfellow,' is a Mediæval personage. He fits the general character assigned to brownies of happily doing small household chores in return for some small generosity like a cup of beer left out for him, though Puck usually has a more mischievous side as well. The word *pixie* is related.

A *barghest* is a spirit, typically taking the form of a huge, fanged, large-clawed black dog (though other shapes and invisible forms are reported as well). It is often conflated with the Grim, an omen of death taking the form of a black dog and haunting cemeteries. The etymology of the name is disputed; many alternate forms also appear, such as *bargeist* and *barguist*.

Bercilak is the latter title character from the famous and unusual Arthurian poem *Sir Gawain and the Green Knight*. He is described there as being not only dressed in green, but wholly green of skin and hair as well; his function seems to be that of a tester of King Arthur's knights, and he is a terrible figure but not an evil one. Though of uncertain meaning, the name *Bercilak* or *Bertilak* may be derived from the Celtic *bresalak*, meaning 'contentious'; his exact significance as a character is disputed, and he is often connected to pre-Christian mythology, Christian folklore of Mediæval Britain, or the devil.

Morgan, or Morgana or Morgan le Fay, was an enchantress in Arthurian myth. Some of the earliest sources for these myths present her fairly neutrally or positively, frequently as a healer; by Malory's time she had become a darker and more hostile character, and in some subsequent versions she is an out-and-out villainess.

ll. 91-94: *valerian*, a fern-like, flowering plant once used in perfumes, was prescribed as a treatment for insomnia as early as the second century. *Lilies* and *irises* are traditional Christian flowers rich in associations, as are roses. All three are used to symbolize the Blessed Virgin Mary, white roses particularly, with the iris (due to its sword-shaped leaves) being specifically symbolic of Mary as the Mother of Sorrows. The lily is also used as a sign of St. Joseph, the Resurrection, and humility.

Juniper (from which gin is derived) was used in Gaelic paganism as an element of rituals designed to cleanse and protect households from malevolent influences.

Holly, which is today mostly associated with Christmas decorations, was given this meaning because its thorn-like leaves and bright red berries were suggestive of Christ's Passion, and, being an evergreen, it would still be flourishing in midwinter. In druidic religion the holly was regarded as a protection against evil spirits.

The *lilac* represents young love and innocence, due to its comparatively early blossoming time.

Buttercups, though beautiful, are highly toxic to horses, cattle, and other livestock.

The *carnation* has a wide range of traditional associations. Purple carnations in particular are linked in English-speaking cultures with capriciousness and unreliability, while in French-speaking cultures they are flowers of ill omen. By contrast, a Christian legend about pink carnations is that they first sprang from the tears shed by the Virgin while she watched Jesus Christ carry the Cross.

l. 106: due to a shift in burial customs, the term is not in common use today, but *barrow* is the native English word for a tumulus or burial mound.

l. 108: *narcissus*, more commonly called daffodils in English, are named for the mythological Narcissus who fell in love with his own reflection and wasted away before it. Narcissus flowers also appear in some versions of the story of the kidnapping of Proserpina by Pluto: Proserpina was taken while gathering flowers, and was picking narcissus when Pluto snatched her.

ll. 126-128: the *apple* has come to be associated in Christian folklore with the forbidden fruit of Eden. It has a long-standing association in much of

European myth with immortality, from Celtic legends to Greek; Avalon, the traditional resting place of King Arthur, literally means *Isle of Apples*. *Bluebells* were sometimes said to be the bells of the fairies.

Hazel was associated with wisdom in Celtic myth. Later stories of witchcraft in Europe reported that wands should by preference be made of hazel wood.

l. 138: *willow* is a traditional symbol of forsaken love. English folklore assigns the willow tree considerable power and malevolence, saying that it can uproot itself and stalk travelers.

l. 139: the *carbuncle* was once thought to be an independent type of stone (now the word is used for any red gemstone, typically a garnet), with magical properties such as shining in the dark; the *Song of Roland* describes the ship of an Islamic emperor setting forth 'with lamps and carbuncles ablaze.'

l. 142: now obsolete, the word *how* was a synonym for *barrow*, sometimes used as a general word for a small hill in northern English dialects. It is chiefly preserved in place names and surnames (often spelled *howe*).

l. 144: *silly* ultimately descends from the Anglo-Saxon *gesælig* meaning 'blessed.' In Middle English the word acquired a much wider range of meanings, from 'good' to 'innocent' to 'weak' to 'pitiful,' before taking on its modern sense of 'laughable, foolish, amusing.' In Mediæval and later folklore, the fairies were sometimes divided into two courts, the Seelie (a Scots variant of the English) and Unseelie: the former could be mischievous and revengeful of injuries, but were generally benignant towards human beings; the latter were hostile, gleefully bringing misfortune on innocent people.

l. 146 *vervain*, or verbena, has long been associated with the supernatural and the magical; in ancient Egypt the plant was referred to as the 'tears of Isis.'

l. 163: *thyme* is a symbol of strength (hence its appearance in the ballad *Scarborough Fair*, where it is supposed to sustain the lovers during their separation).

The *clove* stands for undying love, and its extract was used in Western herbalism as a painkiller.

Barley, in addition to being one of the oldest staple grains cultivated by humans, was also one of the earliest sources of alcohol; indeed, its name may be related to the modern English word *beer*.

ll. 169-170: *basil* has a complex character in folklore. It is sometimes used as a symbol of Satan, and it represented hatred in ancient Greece. Some cultures associate it with lovers, negatively or positively; Keats' poem *Isabella or the Pot of Basil* recounts the tale, told originally by Boccaccio, of a woman who found the head of her murdered lover and kept in in a pot of basil, watering it with her tears.

Parsley, like thyme, appears in the refrain of *Scarborough Fair*, where it symbolizes the removal of bitterness.

Henbane is a poisonous flower of the nightshade family, and has hallucinogenic properties as well. It was used (in conjunction with other traditionally magical herbs like the mandrake) in anæsthetic potions.

Honeysuckle represents devotion; however, it is better known for its marked sweet fragrance. Its blossoms can be picked and their nectar drunk for its honey-like flavor.

l. 184: *ivy* is widely associated with age and decay, due to its tendency to grow on old buildings; some forms are invasive. The plant is also very bitter and toxic.

l. 196: *ivory*, derived usually from the tusks of elephants, has been a prized luxury material since antiquity, and in some places is more highly valued than gold. In Europe it was frequently used to carve religious objects before the trade was banned.

l. 214: *sable* is a heraldic term for black.

l. 224: *foxfire* is a light emitted by certain types of fungus, generally green or bluish-green. Occasionally it can be bright enough to read by.

l. 253: in some stories, fairies cannot abide the sound of bells.

ll. 277-281: the *mandrake* is a poisonous, hallucinogenic plant. Because its root often bears a striking resemblance to the human body, it has long been used in magical practices and had many superstitions associated with it.

Pomegranates, because of their many seeds, are a symbol of eternity. In some versions of the story of Proserpina's abduction by Pluto, the fruit which she ate in the underworld, and by which she was obliged to return there every winter, was identified as a pomegranate.

The *nettle*, though edible, is much better known for its painful, stinging hairs.

Belladonna is more commonly called deadly nightshade. Though it has medicinal and cosmetic uses as well, belladonna is potentially lethal in quantity. It can also cause unpleasant hallucinations and delirium, and was believed in the Middle Ages and early Modern period to be one of the ingredients in witches' flying ointment.

Lovage is an edible plant, the root of which can induce photosensitivity.

Sage is a relative of the psychoactive salvia plant. The Romans used it as a local anæsthetic in classical times.

The *hellebore*, sometimes called the Christmas rose, was used to treat insanity and as an emetic by the ancient Greeks. However, hellebore is also highly toxic, and can cause vertigo, tinnitus, stupor, thirst, swelling, and a sense of suffocation, among its milder symptoms.

Wormwood is the plant from which absinthe is derived. It traditionally stands for sorrow and absence. It also contains the chemical thujone, which can induce convulsions. (The belief that it causes hallucinations, which inspired its romantic reputation in Bohemian culture in the nineteenth and twentieth centuries, has little basis in fact.)

Asphodel was said by Homer to cover the fields of the dead in the underworld. It was often planted on graves.

ll. 294-295: in some traditions, holy things can repel or restrain the fairies. Cold iron is a traditional apotropaic against them, and the rowan was believed to be a powerful protection against malevolent spirits and witches.

ll. 308-310: *rosewood* has long been a prized wood in many countries for its durability, attractive appearance when polished, and persistent fragrance. (The name is derived from the wood's aroma; rosewood plants are actually more closely related to peas than to the true rose.)

Frankincense is an aromatic resin obtained from the olibanum tree and its relatives, growing in the Arabian peninsula. It is commonly used in incense, and best known in the modern West as one of the gifts of the Magi.

Myrrh is another plant used in incenses and perfumes; it also has medicinal properties as an antiseptic and a painkiller. In addition to being brought to Bethlehem by the Magi, it is associated with the Passion, both for its use in embalming and because of its dense thorns.

The *cedar* is an evergreen with richly resinous wood. The cedar of Lebanon is mentioned a number of times in the Bible, being employed in the building of Solomon's Temple and in the ritual of cleansing for recovered lepers.

Rosemary symbolizes remembrance and love. In addition to its appearance in the ballad *Scarborough Fair*, Ophelia mentions its meaning in her monologue on the significances of flowers in *Hamlet*.

Saint John's wort (named for John the Baptist) was believed in some places to ward off fairies and evil forces. In modern times, it has been studied as a possible naturally-occurring antidepressant.

l. 316: the *Angelus* is a Catholic prayer, several hundred years old, combining three Hail Maries with quotations from Scripture. It is traditionally recited at dawn, noon, and dusk.

About the Author

Gabriel Blanchard was born in Japan in 1987, and has since lived in Scotland, California, and the mid-Atlantic. He has been blogging on Christianity, gay issues, the arts, pacifism, and anarchism at Mudblood Catholic since 2013, and has also had essays and reviews published in Crisis, PRISM Magazine, and Pints & Prose. His first book, *Death's Dream Kingdom*, a Victorian gothic novel, was published in 2015. He currently resides in Baltimore, and is definitely not a shaved linsang in a suit pretending to be a human.

More great titles from Clickworks Press
www.clickworkspress.com

The Stone and the Song
Ben Y. Faroe

In a world where words are power and magic is song, a voiceless girl must defeat the sorceress who betrayed her.

"...a magical, timeless realm of dancing statues, gargoyles, and seers. It's the bed time fairy tale we have all been waiting for."

"Narnia fans will be pleased"

Learn more at clickworkspress.com/stoneandsong

The Dagger and the Rose
Bill Hoard

A classic fairy tale about an adopted princess, a kingdom of masked souls, and the search for deep joy and true beauty.

"The Dagger and the Rose [explores] the reality of the princess who is both in need of rescue and responsible for making that rescue possible...Her search for answers, freedom, joy, and beauty are echoes of our longing."

Learn more at clickworkspress.com/daggerandrose.

Also by Gabriel Blanchard

Death's Dream Kingdom
Volume I of The Redglass Trilogy

A young woman of Victorian London has been transformed into a vampire. Can she survive the world of the immortal dead—or, perhaps, escape it?

"The wit and humor are as Victorian as the setting...a winsomely vulnerable and tremendously crafted work of art."

"a dramatic, engaging novel which explores themes of death, love, damnation, and redemption."

Learn more at clickworkspress.com/ddk.

Keep in touch!

Join the Clickworks Press email list and get freebies, production updates, special deals, behind-the-scenes sneak peeks, and more.

Sign up today at clickworkspress.com/join.

www.ingramcontent.com/pod-product-compliance
Lightning Source LLC
Chambersburg PA
CBHW021158080526
44588CB00008B/407